ISBN: 9798813172151
Cover design by: Susan Rose
Editing: Susan Rose

WE LAUGHED, WE CRIED, WE UNDERSTOOD

By Susan Rose
FSAScot

Dedication

To the men of the 4th Royal Tank Regiment

Table of Contents

Chapter 1- pg. 01   Mick has 6 Months.
Chapter 2- pg. 07   On to Leeds
Chapter 3- pg. 11   Bingley Arms
Chapter 4- pg. 13   Power and Control
Chapter 5- pg. 17   Peacocks
Chapter 6- pg. 27   Scarborough Fair
Chapter 7- pg. 37   Royal Armory
Chapter 8- pg. 47   Juicy Bits
Chapter 9- pg. 55   Ribbon Rack
Chapter 10- pg.61   Robinhood's Bay
Chapter 11- pg. 65   Temple Church
Chapter 12- pg. 71   Misfire
Chapter 13- pg. 75   Under Water Detonate
Chapter 14- pg. 81   Belvoir Castle
Chapter 15- pg. 85   Spital Inn
Chapter 16- pg. 87   George Washington
Chapter 17- pg. 93   Departure

Photograph Credits pg. 95

Chapter 1
Mick has 6 Months.

I had been Text Messaging Mick Hardin B.E.M. for 5 years at least every other day. Not once did he mention Cancer. He would talk of his day or funny things about the Royal Tank Regiment/RTR. Just friendly talk, nothing serious ever.

Just friendly chit chat.

"Susan, you need to get over to England as soon as possible," my friend Tom Stewart late of the RTR is texting me from England in May 2017.

Me, "Why?"

"Mick has Terminal Cancer and is not expected to live to the RTR Veterans Get Together in November 2017," replied Tom.

I was to attend that event as the Liaison to the Royal Tank Regiment from Clan Rose.

OMG... my world comes to a complete stop!

"Tom, No!"

"He will not let us visit him, that is why we want you to visit him," replied Tom. "He probably will not let you see him either" says Tom.

"Let me see what I can do," my response.

My Text Message to Mick Hardin "Hey Mick, I am going to be in England for a few days. Can I stop by and say Hi, get Dinner or go to a Pub?"

"Absolutely Susan!" "You can stay at my house, got lots of room." "When are you coming over?" typed Mick.

"I will send you my Travel Info, Dates and Times," "I need to work on my schedule, get back to you soon," from me.

My message to Tom Stewart "He said Yes to me."

This is the year 2017, and terrorists are bombing England, France, and the Netherlands. Cars are being used by terrorist groups to mow people down. At the time "Travel Bans" are being put out by the U.S. Government to restrict travel to London England, Paris France, and the Netherlands. Well, that is just great! How can I get to Leeds England without using the traditional Airline routes?

Think, Think, Think. I had just written a history book about the Norman Vikings, invading England in 1066, William the Conqueror and his Norman Vikings... Vikings, Iceland! An Icelandic Airline had been showing Airline Commercials on TV at the time. "Come Visit Iceland on your way to Europe!"

As the Icelandic Volcano **"Eyjafjallajökull"** had blown up in 2010. Terrorists would not be using Iceland as a port of entry to get to England, as an avenue to bring bombs through. Iceland blows up without any terrorist help at all. That was my thought process anyway. A safe way to arrive in England, via Iceland with decidedly zero terrorist activity.

I flew First Class to Iceland on the advertised Airline. A wonderful flight. Later, while walking around Reykjavik on that flight's layover, I walked past Thor. I am sure it was the Icelandic God, Thor. I stood there with my mouth open staring agog at that guy. He had to be pushing seven feet tall. He walked past, gone before I could pull out my camera.

What was I going to do? Take a picture of a random guy in Iceland? How annoying, glad I only fumbled ineffectually with my camera. How embarrassing. Susan, get your act together.

Icelandic airline flight to Edinburgh, Scotland. As no other Airports were open that were on the OK'd Flights List to England because of the terrorist activities. So, I flew into Edinburgh, Scotland.

The previous evening another Terrorist Attack in Manchester, England the site of a young person's concert. These terrorists were serious.

First Class to Edinburgh and I am the only one in First Class, I am feeling real cool being the only one.

Just Wait! Karma was watching me. Well, the Icelandic airline seems to have upset someone in Edinburgh Airport, as there was no Tube that slides up to the airplane so that customers can walk off into a long tube that is connected to the actual airport building.

Nope.

They wheeled up a metal stairway on wheels for us to climb down. No baggage handlers to remove our luggage to a motorized car that would deliver luggage to one of those handy turnstiles we have in America.

We had to grab our luggage off the ground where it was tossed next to the plane. Really? I stood there all *American,* hands on hips thinking, "I should not be treated this way."

Well, it gets even better. So, I drag my luggage into this Quonset Hut, I follow the line dutifully. I take my luggage to where everyone is putting theirs. By this time, I need to use some facilities, please. Nope. Not going to happen. They want to check our passports first.

I get up to the front of the line. Dancing Slightly. Show the man my Passport with a huge smile.

Now I had just left Iceland, who couldn't have cared less about my Passport.

"The Iceland Official, had asked me why I was showing them my Passport?"

My Answer, "So you can check it and put a stamp in it."

"We do not care about your Passport Mam." Said the Iceland Official.

"Would you like an Iceland Country Stamp?" "I will stamp your Passport for you. What Page would you like it Stamped"? asked the overly polite Iceland Official.

Gee, I felt like a Kindergartener.

Back to the Grumpy man at the Passport Checking Station in Edinburgh Airport in this Quonset Hut off the side of the real Airport. I am sure now that this Quonset Hut is where they place the **Disciplinary Action Needed**, Employees.

I am still dancing. "What is the purpose of your visit to Scotland?" asked the nasty Passport Agent.

"I am not staying in Scotland; I am taking the Train to Leeds England to stay with a friend" I reply.

"Why?" the son of a bitch asks me.

I am dancing faster now. "Because he is sick" says I.

"Are you going to function as his nurse?" Passport Agent.

I am squinting at him now, gritting my teeth. "I will take care of him as needed, as I am not a nurse." I reply.

"Why would you come to see him?" asks the Passport Agent who will be spending his After Life in Hell.

"Because he is dying!" with a glare in my eyes now.

"How did you meet him?"

"Lady, what are the circumstances of your meeting your friend?" Passport man from Hell questions me.

Me, physically I look like every mother/Grandmother type in Scotland. We all have the same physical shape, "Roundish." Reddish Frizzly Hair with a Sweater on. We are an Identifiable Physical Type.

"Scottish Grand Mother"

My Answer "I have to go to the bathroom. But here ya go!"

"OK, I am a Kiltmaker to the Chief of Clan Rose, David Hugh Hariot Baird Rose the 26th Baron of Kilravock. Clan Rose gave permission to the 4th Royal Tank Regiment to wear the Clan Rose Hunting Tartan for their Pipes and Drums.

You know, the Tank Drivers for the UK during Military Actions? Well, they have a Bagpipe Band, they wear the Rose Hunting Tartan. My Friend was their Pipe Major..."

"OK, you can go on through." Agent points behind him.

What he didn't say is, "There is a bathroom right behind you. Then go that way to collect your luggage." No, he did not. I went the way he pointed. Leaving my luggage in the heap of luggage on the Quonset Hut floor. Into the Real Edinburgh Airport, I find relief and go to the Luggage Turn Style area.

Nothing, no Luggage.

I ask the Question-and-Answer person, "Where is the Luggage for the Iceland Airlines?"

Answer, "Oh No, you are supposed to bring it with you, from the plane."

And

"No, you cannot go back behind the gate and retrieve it" replied the Answer Person.

Bribery!

Bribery is how to get my luggage that I left on the Quonset Hut floor. Yes, I bribed an airport worker person to find my luggage and bring it back to me. Yes, this seems to me to be a questionable way to get past officials during a time of Terrorist Attacks, but I had a train to catch, going south.

Chapter 2
On to Leeds

I locate the bus to the Train Station. Taking a deep breath, I clear my thoughts. I am on a mission, "To Mick." I have my train schedule and for some magical reason I am on time. I take the Express Train to Leeds, England.

I call Mick to meet me at the Station at the specified time. Lovely, four and ½ hours racing through Scotland and England. Beautiful Scenery.
Thinking to myself, do I really look like a terrorist? Maybe I should work on my personal style from now on. An elderly Scottish Grandmother Type seems to be a very Dangerous Look. All Passport Agents seemingly are looking to stop! Wow.

This Express Train seemed to have set a Land Speed Record for trains. Way ahead of schedule. But that's OK. Because Leeds Train Station is a Rabbit Warren of confusing racks of metal rail stairs and metal rail pass ways. I finally found the right way to the main Landing of the Station.

I am about 1 story up, I see Mick. I started yelling his name. He sees me and smiles and waves. Mick looks ailing, he has a huge Jacket on, that in his current state is now too big for his frame.

We drag my luggage to the front entrance and walk to where he thinks his taxi is waiting. No Taxi. We stand waiting for it to show back up. Nothing. The Taxi is 2 cars down from where we are standing. The driver finds us.

Thinking to myself, from here on out I will be the navigator while here. No problems…

Laughing. No problems whatsoever.

Pulling up to his home he says to me, he doesn't have women to his home. I am the first woman to be invited into his home.

Hmm…? OK.

His home is a 2 story walk up, wood and plaster home. His yard was OK but neglected surrounded by a low chain link fence. Possibly a condo. In what appears to be a small community of houses the same as one another.

I drag my stuff up to my appointed second floor bedroom. Nice. I go sit back down in the front room.

I am looking around his front room. Everything is 4th RTR. Pictures, a Silver Tank, pictures of the Regiment, of the Queen. Cards from his large family were just what I had expected to see.

Mick comes in and sits down exhausted.

"Mick, when was the last time you ate? I am starving!" I ask.

"3 days ago, he answers."

"Oh no! I am thinking. Why haven't you eaten in 3 days?"

His answer is "It makes me throw up."

"Are you drinking any liquid food supplement?"

"No." said Mick.

This is serious. In mom mode now.

"What kind of food do you like?"

"Oriental Food." Says Mick.

"No way, that would bounce back up quickly. What other food do you like?" I ask.

"How about Chicken or Turkey and Potatoes, Vegetables?" me.

He says, "The Carvery!"

I have zero idea what a "Carvery" is, but I have got to get nourishment into Mick as soon as possible. We grab a Taxi and set off to the local "Carvery."

I go in and see what Carvery is offering. It is Thanksgiving Dinner to us Americans! I was under the mistaken conclusion that Americans invented Thanksgiving Dinner. The English can have that meal every day of the week.

Americans can have it once maybe twice a year.

Thanksgiving Dinner is never thrown up. It seems to be impossible to throw up Turkey, Stuffing, Potatoes, Green Beans and Gravy after eating. It sits in your stomach like a soft lump, perfect. Mick had ½ a plate full. We go back to his house, go to our separate rooms, and fall asleep.

Mick has zero repeats of his dinner backing up. Excellent

Chapter 3
Bingley Arms

The next day Mick wants to take me to The Bingley Arms, the oldest Pub in England. So, we set off in his little car, Mick driving. There is no way that I can drive in the UK. It terrifies me. I am literally screaming watching traffic coming at his little car. I am sure we will be dead from a head on collision. So, I decide to just look at Mick's face and talk to him as he drives. Safer for all concerned.

I like to fix problems, especially my own.

Mick tells me about the Bingley Arms and how old it is. In America I say that we tear anything old down and replace it with something new. But our construction is not of Stone, but wood. Which has a limited life. The Bingley Arms is a stone building with a very low front door. People seemed to be shorter back in the day. It is the first very old building I have been in, so what did I know?

It is pouring down rain. No worries, this is what I had expected the weather to be in England. So, I was content. Smiling listening to Mick talk about this and that. Just friends talking. He wants to show me the Yorkshire Dales. He has a look-out site, to see his **perfect** view of Yorkshire.

Off we go up the street to an area set up for
Teaching the Art of Stacked Stone Fences that
are so famous in Yorkshire. Seems to be a great
thing to learn if your land is full of Stones,
anyway it's his perfect site for a viewing.

We walked to the ledge formed by two giant
stones, which could be sat upon while looking at
the gorgeous scenery. Problem, the winds are
howling, and the rain is driving down sideways.
His umbrella blows inside out.
Like a scene from a movie.
I started laughing, he starts laughing, and it was
a delight.
We drove back home laughing.

Chapter 4
Power and Control

On the drive back to his home, I ask Mick if he knows why the Royal Tank Regiment wears the Rose Hunting Tartan? No, is his answer.

Hmmm, its "Power and Control." I say.
.

The Clan Rose Chief, Hugh Rose the 24th was in real life the Lt. Col. Hugh Rose of Kilravock 1863-1946 Commanding 1st Battalion Black Watch. Hugh Rose the 24th knew most of the History of the deRos Family, but he had not uncovered my discovery of the Robert II Furfan de Ros.

His only son Hugh Rose the Heir Apparent was killed in El-Alamein #2 during the Attack by Rommel.

This Hugh Rose the 24th was a Lt. Col. And stationed in Malta as an advisor during both World Wars so Field Marshal Bernard Law Montgomery of the Eighth Army and the Royal Tank Regiment would have known him personally.

I tell Mick that I have researched and verified a 1000 Year Timeline of the de Ros/Rose Family. Going back prior to the 1066 Invasion of England by William the Conqueror.

5 deRos brothers were in the Invasion Force.

That I know the names of deRos Castles prior to the Invasion of 1066. The foundation Ancestor of the Kilravock Roses was also one of the 25/26 Sureties of the Magna Carta, his name was Robert II "Furfan" deRos. He lived in Yorkshire by the way.
Mick was stunned.

Well, how about I tell you my stories about the de Ros/Roses and then you tell me about the RTR and the pictures of you trying not to laugh just before those pictures being taken, OK?
He was just now understanding that there is a whole back story to Clan Rose of Kilravock. I could see him making connections in his head as to the "Why?" of the choice of the Rose Hunting Tartan. It seemed to make even more sense to him, with the "Rest of the Story" so to speak.
We got back to his home. Would you like to go to my private Pub? It's just up the street. Are you kidding me? Ask practically any American that question, and 99 % of them will say Of Course! And we did.
We had eaten in a Carvery Restaurant before we got home. Another Thanksgiving Dinner that could not be beat. Why mess with success?
We walk up the street, four houses cross the street up on the corner. A Pub in your own neighborhood!

I was raised in the country on an Arabian Horse Farm, miles from town in the outback of California. Most of the streets of Valley Center, California (the real Old West) were at that time dirt. Everywhere was a drive. 45 minutes one way minimum. What a delight to be able to walk 4 house widths and arrive at your destination.

We walk in and the patrons turn as one, to see who came in.

"Hello! I say quite loudly with a wave."

We walked to the bar and the gal bar tender is a youngish 30. Dressed very casual no Uniform, asked what I wanted? She already knew what Mick wanted. I ordered a Mout Cider with Berries. She grabbed a glass; I said no glass just the bottle. Don't want a glass. The attendees laugh and say I am a player! The patrons of the Pub are work-a-day types or newly retired average Joes.

"I ask Mick what his doctor says he can drink?" "Anything I want says, Mick" As it should be at this stage in his game. We sit comfortably by ourselves, and the others played games like Darts and Pool. We didn't pay much attention to the other guys. There were no women inside but me and the Bar Tender. The bar closes at 11:30 so we walk down to his place 4 doors down on the right. We are getting along as the old friends that we were. Just pals, nothing hidden. Equals.

We get back to his house, he asks me if I had seen the movie "Me Before You?"
"No, I had not heard of it."

"Would you please watch it with me tonight?" says Mick.
It was late but why not?
"Sure." From me.

It is a story of a girl/woman who is hired to look after a dying man. They become fast friends and then he dies.
I went through a paper towel roll and a toilet paper roll to watch the movie. Sobbing, I got the Hurky Jerky Sobbing Tears while I was Crying. I am a mess. End of Movie.

I look over at Mick, who is not teary eyed at all.
"I ask him if I am the female character in the movie?"

"Yes, you are." Confirms Mick.

That character's job in the movie was to lift the spirits of the dying man. The movie seems to be about us. Me and Mick except for we are much older, and we have been friends a long time.

So, then I knew the roles we are to be playing in real life for 10 days.

And no, I did not make that up.

Seems Mick had put a lot of planning into our visit together.

Chapter 5
Peacocks

Let's go for a drive tomorrow, ahh… today, OK? Off to bed and we rise at 10 am. Refreshed. Mick again has a very peaceful night, no vomiting no pain.

"Have you ever been to Rievaulx Abbey in Yorkshire?" I ask.
"It was controlled by Robert II Furfan de Ros as a Knights Templar."

"No, I was in the military we didn't visit places, we were assigned places. I have never been anywhere in Yorkshire. I have only looked at it from the site that I took you to." Responds Mick.

We have this conversation as we gather our coats, we decide to have a small breakfast on the road.
As opposed to Whitby Abbey with its stacked Stone construction Rievaulx Abbey has Construction Style used in the Middle East. Meaning the construction of this Abbey occurred after the 1st Crusade.

I am not pushing for Mick's stories; he knows why I have been sent. To get his stories. Here is the thing, he wants my stories first.
Stingy Man…
I smile at him. I have time.

We drive up to Rievaulx Abbey, entrance.
Marked by a grinding stone with the name
Rievaulx in metal Letters.

Up on the hill to the right is a magnificent ruin,
is the only description for Rievaulx Abbey. We
walk to the Museum's Tea Counter and order
ourselves Tea. We sit and have Breakfast
Muffins and Tea, while looking up the hill at the
Abbey in Ruins. Big Glass windows are the walls
of the Tea Room and Museum, so any which way
we turn there are magnificent views.

King Henry VIII that evil, evil man.

To purposely destroy works of art that were the Abbeys, Churches, and Cathedrals. What a shame! The easiest way to destroy something as big as an Abbey is to pull the lead off of the roof. The lead kept the moisture from pouring onto the woodwork. Without the lead the wood would rot, and the building would cave in on itself.

As I will have future contact with the Manners Family concerning their connection to the deRos family. This does not look favorably on Thomas Manners the Earl of Rutland. This was posted outside of Rievaulx Abbey itself.

THE END OF MONASTIC LIFE AT RIEVAULX

Rievaulx fell victim to Henry VIII's destruction of the monasteries. The official reason was that monks no longer kept their religious observances, but in reality the king had political and economic motives.

The abbey was suppressed in December 1538. The monks were cast out but received pensions. Rievaulx was sold to Thomas Manners, earl of Rutland, though the plate, bells and lead from the roofs were reserved for the king.

Documents prepared at this time describe Rievaulx's buildings and precincts. It is clear that Manners was determined to extract everything of value from the former monastery, which was stripped of its contents and rapidly reduced to ruins.

Mick, I yell! Come see this, Peacock!

"So? He says," questioning my sanity.

I tell him my business motto as a Kiltmaker is: "A Celtic Peacock Enabler". I dress Scottish Drum Majors, when dressed to perfection they have a swagger to their step. With the pleats in the back of their kilt swaying. Kind of like how a Peacock shows of his Tail Feathers."

These are stone peacocks. Mick then sneaks my camera behind the glass wall and snaps pictures of the stone Peacocks.

Mick laughs at my teary eyes about the peacocks. He Says, "Of Course you would have a predilection to Peacocks!"

"It Runs in the family."

The Stone Carved 900-year-old Peacock of Rievaulx Abbey. Why the peacocks? Upon researching the use of Peacocks, they are a Symbol of The Knights Templar. You have them somewhere about your home or embroidered on your clothing, it then is a sign that other Templars will see that you are a Templar as well. We hiked up to the Abbey. Mick is thunder struck at the beauty of the Abbey. He was amazed by the layout of it. It had a running toilet facility by way of a small river that was channeled through the Abbey's underground. Smart. He was struck that he had never heard of this Abbey, being that it is so close to his house. I only snapped a couple of pictures of Mick as he didn't want pictures of him in Cancer Mode.

To me he looked just fine.
Next, we drive further up the hill to Helmsley Castle and the surrounding town of Helmsley. I tell Mick, Helmsley Castle was Robert II Furfan de Ros's first castle, he goes on to own five. Four in England and one in Scotland. Helmsley Castle has an amazing history.

It is mentioned in Beowulf. That's right.

Exactly who do you have to be, to own the Castle mentioned in the poem Beowulf?

Think that through for a bit. It's called Power and Control!

At the main gate to Helmsley Castle are Viking Men, Modern Art Metal Sculptures standing in threatening postures.

In defense of the Castle Gate of Helmsley.
Yes, the Town of Helmsley is very proud of its connection to Beowulf. As a military man Mick was extremely interested in the Defending Viking Warriors.

There is still a partial manor house standing that I wanted to tour. Mick said he would rather look at the defenses and the still existing stone cannon balls that were used to blow apart Helmsley Castle.

I am not sure if this is the exact Cannon Ball or a Trebuchet Ball used in the destruction of Helmsley Casttle.

Robert II Furfan de Ros sometimes his name was spelled Roos. No standardazation of spelling untill mid 1400s. Plus I do believe the above pictured Templar is actually Robert II furfan de Ros's Great Uncle Hugh de Payens actually. Picture next page.

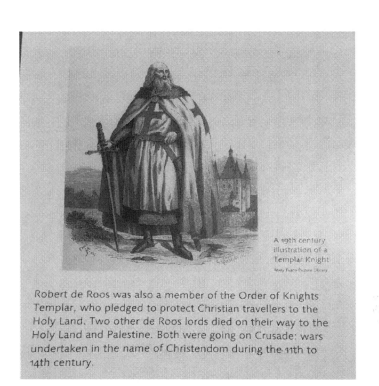

A 19th century illustration of a Templar Knight

Mary Evans Picture Library

Robert de Roos was also a member of the Order of Knights Templar, who pledged to protect Christian travellers to the Holy Land. Two other de Roos lords died on their way to the Holy Land and Palestine. Both were going on Crusade: wars undertaken in the name of Christendom during the 11th to 14th century.

The back enterence to Helmsley Castle.

Looking out of the remaining structure of Helmsley Castle to a beautiful portion of a Castle wall still standing.

Chapter 6
Scarborough Faire

Then on to Scarborough Castle and Sea Port. Yes, this was a big, long day for Mick, but he was game. He could see what I was trying to show him the Power and Control of the de Ros/Rose Family.

This site is a Port and Castle found on the North Sea on the East Coast of Yorkshire. In History Piers/Peter deRos in the early 1100's controlled this port. Piers was the,

Great Grand Father of Robert II Furfan deRos. Foundation Ancestor to the Kilravock Roses.

Mick sat in the car while I scouted the Castle and Port.

The village of Scarborough is quaint and picturesque.

Remains of Scarborough Castle

Going to Scarborough Faire, "Parsley Sage Rosemary and Tyme" 1966 Song by Simon and Garfunkel, The Lyrics were written hundreds of years ago, consisting of impossible tasks for lovers to attempt, to earn each other's True Love.

A portion of the tune, as I understand it, is in reference to a Faire held at Scarborough Castle after the ships came into the port of Scarborough. The Faire was to sell goods from the ships that came in bearing European products plus a time for joining with friends to socialize.

Yes, the deRos's knew how to throw a Fine Party. Since we still are singing about it, must have been a great time had by all.

Simon and Garfunkel, A Music Duo.
"Parsley, Sage, Rosemary and Thyme" 1966
Remember it? Sing along with me:

"Are you going to Scarborough Faire?
Parsley, Sage, Rosemary, and Thyme
Remember me to one who lives there
She once was a true love of mine"

The de Ros/Rose connection to events through the last 1,000 years of UK History is stunning. In my research, the deRos/Rose Family were part of almost every significant event that occurred.

Meaning they were high up in the Peerage for almost 1000 years.

Power and Control...

Then, as you can read, my trip was 2-fold.

Get stories from Mick Hardin B.E.M. Plus, continue doing my research on the de Ros/Rose Family of Kilravock, that Gifted the Rose Hunting Tartan to the 4th Royal Tank Regiment.

Pictured is Lady Elizabeth Rose the 25th Baroness of Kilravock, receiving her Medal for the Gift of the Rose Hunting Tartan for the 4th Royal Tank Regiment to use and be worn by the Pipes and Drums of the 4th Royal Tank Regiment.

An image of what the Uniform was to look like using the Rose Hunting Tartan for the Royal Tank Regiment. Artist Simon Dyer.

For Major Gordon Grey (OC G Sqn) in 1973 as to what the Pipe Major would look like.

Look closely for the painted on Chinese Eyes. One of the Projects Mick and I worked on when we were not driving about. Was research as to the Why of the Chinese Eyes?

Seems that in WWI the Tank drivers crashed the Tanks often. Doing damage to the tanks or getting the tracks torn off. It was determined that Chinese Metal Workers were needed to repair the Metal Tanks. After the Chinese repaired the damage of the crashed Tanks, that were not damaged in acts of War but crashed as the guys were not adept at driving yet.

As cars had just been invented and most Tankies then, didn't own a car yet. The Chinese metal workers painted Chinese Eyes on the forward portion of the tank, so that the eyes would aid the Tank Drivers with improved navigational skills.
Nice of them.

Mick next to the Danish Mermaid by Edvard
Erikson at the Langelinie Promenade
Copenhagen, Denmark.

Mick in Pipe Major mode in front of a Tank.

Oh, what a time they had. **Relax Guys** he didn't tell me what you all got up to in South America.

Mick would only tell me some of his stories, Not All.

On Tour in South America. Mick is standing on the left.

Chapter 7
Royal Armory

"Mick, is it making more sense about the "Power and Control" of Clan Rose?" I ask.

"Yes, it is making more and more sense," from Mick. "Nothing to be ashamed of there," his words. He had the right of it. The 4th Royal Tank Regiment is all about Power and Control, which is what the Tanks are used for in military action Power and Control. The next day Mick has a doctor appointment in Leeds.

"I ask Mick if he would like me to sit in the doctor's office and wait for him?"

"No, no you should visit the Royal Armory Museum in Leeds" while I am at the appointment."

He dropped me off first then went on to his doctor appointment.

The Leeds Royal Armory on the River Aire.

Leeds looks to have been a heavy manufacturing town. To move heavy manufactured goods, it was easier to put the goods on a canal boat and float it where you needed it.

I walked about the Leeds Royal Armory Museum fascinated by all the detail that was put into every display. For the Elephants for a display, they used real Elephants Taxidermized, same with the Horse and Lions. So that the armor was showed off as to how it was used correctly.

The action of this display is exactly as it would

have been if it was real life. The only things that are not real are the depicted humans.

The horses are also Taxidermized, meaning that these horses were at some time, real. The horses had to be more than 20 hands tall. For a horse that is extremely tall.

So 20 Hands X 4 Inches = 6.6666 feet tall.

I walked until I found a display on the Angincourt Battle 1415. Seems a de Ros relative named Lord John Roos participated in it.

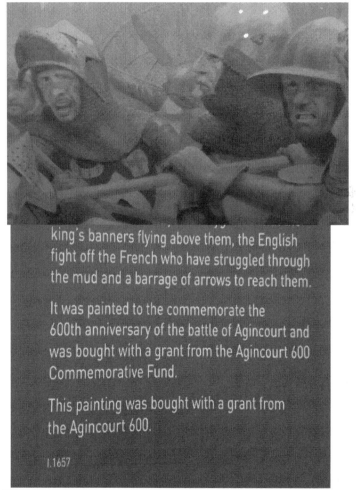

king's banners flying above them, the English fight off the French who have struggled through the mud and a barrage of arrows to reach them.

It was painted to the commemorate the 600th anniversary of the battle of Agincourt and was bought with a grant from the Agincourt 600 Commemorative Fund.

This painting was bought with a grant from the Agincourt 600.

I.1657

The Battle of Agincourt 1415, last battle of the 100 Years War.

See red line to the head of Lord John Roos.

1. **King Henry V**
   - victor of Agincourt

2. **Humphrey, Duke of Gloucester**
   - brother of Henry V, wounded

3. **Edward, Duke of York**
   - commander, killed

4. **John, Lord Roos**

5. **Sir Thomas Erpingham**
   - commander

6. **Sir John Cornewall**
   - commander

7. **Sir Robert Babthorpe**
   - controller of the King's Household

8. **Sir Thomas Strickland**
   - bearer of the Standard of St. George

9. **Personal Standard of Henry V**

10. **Arms of St Edmund and St Edward the Confessor**

11. **Arms of the Holy Trinity**

Looking up the Tower Room in the Armory

The Gifted Helmet for King Henry VIII from the King of Germany.

He looks to have had a sense of humor. As there is welded on snot dripping out of the nose...
The Royal Armory in Leeds is just amazing, no other words can describe the details of the work that went into all the displays. Everything gorgeously displayed.

The Armory is a modern steel and glass frame tower where the hand-to-hand combat weapons are displayed in fascinating patterns rising 6 stories. Then a huge metal frame building making a square box for 5 stories. Each level being 6 meters tall.

I locate a large painting of the Battle of Agincourt dated October 25, 1415. Agincourt Battle was the last battle of the Hundred Year War between England and France. England won with fewer men.

Surprisingly towards the center of this painting is the figure of John Lord Roos (Spellings Varied for de Ros) alongside #1 King Henry V, #2 Duke of Gloucester, #3 Duke of York then #4 John Lord Roos, on a list of 8 Noted Peers. He is mentioned 4th.

"Catch a cab back to my house after you are done. I will be too tired to pick you up after my appointment." Says Mick.

Not sure of the time that Mick will be done at the doctor's appointment.
I hail a Water Taxi on the River Aire that flows alongside the Armory Museum. I notice that this is the way to get around the City of Leeds. As the Freeways are circular surrounding Leeds.
Whereas the Rivers and Canals go directly to an organized spot on the map. The Canals obviously came first and the Freeways hundreds of years later. Canal cruising an enjoyable way to waste time.

Arriving back at Mick's home by Taxi, Mick has no energy to walk up to the Pub.

Chapter 8
Juicy Bits

The next day Mick wants to take me to his Yorkshire Dales Observation Site/Stack Stone Fence Learning Center, as it is a lovely day with no rain.

I start asking Mick about the pictures of him concerning events with the RTR. I am going to ask him about his Stories now. It is time...

Guess not.

He quickly deviates onto a gravel road in the middle of nowhere. This is not the way we went last time to the Overlook.

Mick said "You need to Play it Cool. Are You Game? We very possibly could be arrested."

"What???"

My head snaps up, concentrating now! Well, I have traveled halfway around the world by myself. So, to not be game now, would be just stupid, as far as I am concerned. He turns into a large Satellite Facility Operated by the U.S. Military in Yorkshire. We drive in a bit and two very well armed soldiers approach Mick's Vehicle, asking for our business?
"Sorry, Mick says I must have turned the wrong way down the road."

We leave the Base, Mick bursts into laughter.

And says, "It gets them every time!"

My guess is they have a photograph on the wall of their office of Mick's Little Car. As this couldn't have been the only time he had done this stunt.

Nut…

He discussed his ex-wife and kids on this drive. I just listened, no Judgement. My perspective on Mick's personal life was, the 4th RTR was first and foremost in his priorities. As it should be with an Officer.

Sorry ladies his job was to watch over, train and "Keep Safe" his men. Next was, to have the Best Damned Pipe Band in the Military. Period.

Seems his wife had no interest in either one of his top two priorities in life.

We arrive at Mick's Look-Out/Stack Stone Fence Building Learning Center. It's a glorious Day, the views out to Yorkshire Dales and beyond are like out of a Disney Cartoons, so beautiful it looks fake. Deep lush green pastures, separated by long and winding Stack Stone Fences, darling little Stone Cottages in and amongst winding roads.

I am positive that Disney animators were supplied pictures of the Dales to put into the early cartoons. Mick gets a picture of me seated on the giant edge stones with the Yorkshire Dales as the background. He was so proud of his Look-Out site.

I am interested in getting the Stories to the pictures that I have, that show Mick "Almost Laughing," or "Smiling and the Person behind him glaringly Mad," or "Huge smile shaking the hand of Queen Elizabeth II," or "Smirking, with everyone else Laughing Uncontrollably" or "Group Photos of the RTR" and "a couple of snaps, no one smiling at all."

This is why Tom Stewart texted me. It's for me to get these stories. It's Time.

I would hold up a picture, Mick would smile and chuckle.

I will start with Mick's most famous photograph of all time. As this is the one everyone asks about.
He set the scene as no other could do. I was transfixed. Come on... what happened?

Well, we were at a Base in Germany at a Regimental Pipe Band Competition. The Bands were all lined up for the Awards Ceremony. We had performed earlier in the day in front of a set of Pipe Band Judges. The RTRPB (RTR Pipe Band) is on the left side facing the Grandstand with all the other Bands lined up to our right.

In front of us are photographers located between the Regiments and the Grandstand but much closer to the Regiments than the Grandstand. Coincidentally the Queen is in a private box in the Grandstand. No secret. We are to show respect at all times, so no smiling, serious only, business there.

Anyways this one photographer, a woman in a very short skirt (this is the 80's) is squatting down to take pictures of all the Bands that are lined up. She does not put her knee down, just squats, with knees wide open with no underwear on. Now we are UK Military Regiments, part of our look is to be serious and look tough. No smiles allowed, ever.

This woman photographer is working her way down the different Regiments in line, the RTR is last. I am in front of the RTRPB, and I can see this crazy woman photographer flashing each Pipe Band as she works her way towards our end of the line. She is obviously flashing the Bands as it is so deliberate. She knows we cannot react to what she is doing.

I just could not let this go! She gets in front of my men. I use my Pipe Major's Tone of Voice quite loud.

"MADAME!!! ARE YOU AWARE? ... THAT WE... ALL... CAN SEE... YOUR JUICEY BITS???"
Pandemonium broke out in the Ranks. Literally Every Soldier of every band **Burst Out Laughing**. We the RTRPB step off to collect our award that was just awarded to us, as I spoke those Words!

No, the Queen did not hear me, or if she did, she did not acknowledge it. That photograph of that incident made all the newspapers. So, I am sure the Queen saw the Newspaper, as that picture was the front page above the fold.

God, I so loved this man. If I was in the Military, I would want this guy to be my Commanding Officer.

Back to his home, another Thanksgiving Dinner at the Carvery "That could not be beat." Reference to the Arlo Guthrie Tune "Alice's Restaurant" Yes, we sang tunes that we knew, while we drove about.

We walked up to the Pub. I am met with a Chorus of... SUSAN!!! As I entered the pub seemed they had been waiting for us. I am getting to know his mates from the Pub. I can now tease and laugh with them.

One of his mates has such a heavy accent that I cannot decipher one word he says. So, I Grab a hold of his lapels, comically shake him violently side to side, look him square in the eyes and say,

"SPEAK ENGLISH!"

The Pub erupts in laughter! My God Mick, "She is Hilarious!
I have learned from the Master.

We toddle back down to his house. Mick salutes his neighbor's top window. I look up and see nothing.

"Who was that?" I question.
"Oh! My Dad," replies Mick
"Are you serious? Your Dad?" I question?
"Yep, my dad," chuckles Mick.

Mick is around 68 at that point in time. Quick calculations in my head. So, Daddy is roughly 88 years old. OK...

Now I had been coming and going from Mick's house without a care for days. Not thinking anyone would be on the lookout for Mick's activities or house guests. But his dad? Yikes! Wait we are both older and Mick is very sick nobody would think???

I started laughing.

Mick had planned my visit to a "T".

Nothing to chance.

Chapter 9
Ribbon Rack

A no travel day today. I cannot just sit and contemplate the world. I must be doing something, always.

"Mick, how is your Ribbon Rack?" I inquire.

"Oh, its fine, don't worry your head about my medals." Mick

"Get it out, you said you have a meeting that you need to wear it to."

"I am a Kiltmaker for a profession, I know that Piper's Pipes destroy anything on their chests."

So, I figure Mick's Ribbon Rack is not going to be at its best. I was right.

"Wow, what did you spill on this?" I ask.

"Do you have a Regimental Tie that is in better condition than this?" Oh, My Goodness, his Tie is not salvageable either.

"Mick, what do you have to shine these Medals up with?" I ask.

I walk into his kitchen to look for silver polish and find another surprise.

"My God! Mick! What is this???"

He had been standing right behind me waiting for a reaction.

A giant photograph of a Topless Woman Dancing along in front of Mick Hardin Piping in what looks to be a Bar. It's huge! The dimensions would be for a Public Bar with very tall walls.

Mick laughs, "Saying it had been hanging in the "Chequers," that his dad ran."

"Chequers! Wow!"
"Yes, My Dad had to have this photograph on the wall of Chequers."
"So, you get this crazy funny personality that is you Mick, from your dad?' I asked.

"Yes, I am afraid so," he replied.

We both laugh. That guy in the upstairs window next door is responsible for the guy Mick had become. Bless his dad.

Shaking my head and smiling, now on to shining his medals.

We tear them apart, there is literally no saving the Ribbons.

"Do you have a Local Phone Book, to look for a Military Uniforms Cleaning and Corrections?" I ask.
Yes, He makes an appointment to get a new Ribbon Rack. We set to shining up his Medals. I have a go at polishing, really to no success. Mick starts in on them and creates perfection within minutes, after years of neglect. They are ready to be dropped off for new ribbons and a new rack. We placed an order for a New Regimental Tie. We look over his suits and make sure they are above par.

"He says he should tell me about his Medals, He has one for Northern Ireland, his face changes and he says he is not ever going to speak of Northern Ireland."

I ask about the photographs with the "Unsmiling" pictures. "Was that in Northern Ireland during the Troubles?" "I will not speak to you, about Northern Ireland."
Understood. No means No. I will never ask about Northern Ireland again period.
Changing the subject of his Medals.
Mick tells me about becoming a Piper in the Military. OK, that will be safe. His answer was,
"My Commanding Officer needed more Pipers for his Pipe Band. He told me to learn the Bagpipes, or I was going to get the worst assignments possible if I didn't. Well, I had witnessed him in action against my fellow enlisted mates. I chose to learn the Pipes as fast and be as good as I possibly could."
Mick played in the Scots Guards before he was recruited to the 4th RTR. With a leaning to be a player in the 4th RTR Pipe Band as his reason for moving to the Tank Regiment.

In the 4th RTRPB, Mick replaced Pipe Major Elder, as the new Pipe Major. So, he was way better than a good Bagpiper, he was one of the Best. While in the Scots Guards he had also become highly proficient as a Highland Dancer. He was responsible then to teach the 4th RTR to Highland Dance as well.

"So, Mick where were you born? And a Highland Dancer too? With no Scottish Accent!" He evades my question and changes to an answer of what he wants to tell me.

Knowing I was going to be writing his Stories.

"Well, I had been out visiting my friends, messing about. I ran out of money. I had nothing to eat and couldn't pay my rent. Not even bus fare.
A recruiting office was just right there in front of me. The military recruiter said they would support all my needs, so I joined up. As there were zero jobs where I lived, I was an all-in kind of guy, so into the Military I went."
Speak to me about your BEM Honor.
What was this honor for?
"I taught local kids to the Base in Germany where the 4th RTR was located at the time, to Highland Dance. They organized into a Highland Dance troupe and performed with the 4th RTR Pipe Band when we performed. Rose Hunting Tartan on the Dancers too."

A BEM Honor is a British Empire Medal, it is a British and Commonwealth award for Meritorious civil or military service worthy of recognition by the Crown. The Current honour was created in 1922 to replace the original medal, which had been established in 1917 as part of the Order of the British Empire.

The CLAN ROSE HIGHLAND DANCERS - BRD

"Susan, as I am to be dying soon. I would like you to take my Copy of the Citation for the BEM Honour back to America with you. I want you to keep it safe."

My mouth open, looking at Mick. "I am serious Susan."   "OK Mick."

On to another Thanksgiving Dinner that couldn't be beat. Then our walk up to his local Pub.

We spoke of his future treatments for his Cancer. I told him of my bout with Breast Cancer in 2005/2006. That my father had died of Pancreatic Cancer in 2007. I asked Mick about his prognosis. He said he was terminal. This I already knew...

Yes that is a picture of Mick as a small boy in a kilt. Another Picture of Mick as a Scots Guards Piper.
That he was going to start up Chemo again real soon. I asked if his next Chemo would possibly change his outcome?
"No."

We had a heart-to-heart conversation about our combined Chemo and Radiation treatments. Just relating what we both knew of those subjects.

Chapter 10
Robinhood's Bay

The next day Mick wants to drive to Whitby Abbey. On the coast of the North Sea at the end of Yorkshire north of Scarborough Castle. Then return to Scarborough to see if we can get inside Scarborough Castle itself.

At Whitby Abbey, Mick follows behind me taking pictures of me while I photographed the Abbey. Why Not... I did not have the right to tell him not to. I just smile.

Whitby Abbey on the North Yorkshire Coast of the North Sea.

Leaving Whitby Abbey, we pulled into Robin Hood's Bay. Yes, there is such a place. No Robin Hood was never there. It's where smugglers landed their contraband goods and smuggled them ashore.

As far as I am concerned it is the most beautiful site in all of England. It is breathtaking scenery.

Our view down to Robinhood's Bay from our Picnic Table.

So much so that the place was packed, zero parking. "No Way", not as far as I was concerned. "Mick, pull up to that little Antique Hotel that is so beautiful, yes that one."

"Susan, we cannot park there; it is posted for Hotel Guests Only."

"Look here Mick. I am an American Right? All English people know that Americans are pushy asshats and obnoxiously will not obey parking rules, right?" I asked him.

Mick laughed and responded, "Well, Yes!"

"Then pull into that restricted Parking Lot and park. If we get hassled tell them I was driving, that you could not convince the American that parking was not allowed."

He laughed and followed orders. We went into the Bakery in front of the Hotel and got a couple of Pastries and a Couple of Ciders, went outside sat at a picnic table and enjoyed the view.

We sat for an hour while I waxed poetic on my favorite subject, Robert II Furfan de Ros. The foundation Ancestor to the Roses of Kilravock and is fundamentally why the RTR wears the Rose Hunting Tartan, to this day.

Mick spoke of his men of the 4th RTR Pipe Band.

We left our illegal parking space without worry or harassment from the Hotel Management. Headed toward Scarborough Castle again but too late to go inside. We had gathered too much wool on that picnic table in front of the Antique Hotel above Robin Hoods Bay.

Chapter 11
Temple Church

I am bound for London on a south bound Train. Mission: to find Temple Church, said to be just off Fleet Street, London. Through an arched walkway, seems you must know where you are going, as you would never just happen to walk past Temple Church.

The Round of Temple Church

Robert II Furfan de Ros listening intently to me.

He was a might handsomer prior to the work

done on him by a man who claimed to know how to clean ancient Effigies, but that is another story altogether.

Look closely you can see the
Trois Bouts D'Leau on his shield?

I was to be touring Tower Church, then head
back to Leeds, get a taxi back to Mick's House in
one day, no overnight stay.
I found Temple Church, and it is much smaller
than I thought it would be. Roughly twice the
size of my own home back in California. So,
Very, Very Small.

I enter and say To the Ticket Taker that I have a
Relative lying in Effigy. That I would like to have
a word with him, please. The attendant was
startled, looked at me and saw that I was
smiling. He sold me a ticket; I went inside. I
could not quite get out of my head how small the
place was.
History books have claimed that King John
during the Magna Carta Time lived in the
Temple Church for safety. Wait a minute. A King
does not just stay in a Tiny Church by his own
wish. To my mind, King John was incarcerated
by the Templars of Temple Church.
I will research this idea very well, inside, and
out, every which way and write about it in
another book that I go on to publish in 2020.
"The Knights Templar Hiding in Plain Sight, The
Life of Robert II Furfan de Ros."

Yes, he is the foundation ancestor of the Roses
of Kilravock and is laying in Effigy in Temple
Church to the Right Hand of William Marshall.
That's right.

To the Right Hand of William Marshall!
Mmmm? Power and Control, Yes!

I have my talk with the stone Effigy of Robert II Furfan de Ros. I update him on all things "Rose of Kilravock". He and I concluded that I was correct about everything I have uncovered so far about the de Ros family, Robert II agrees with me.
As he should…
I also photograph everything.
A little side note, During the bombing of London by the Nazi's in WWII, Temple Church did sustain damage to the roof of Temple Church.
The roof later dropped down on the Effigies.
My, Robert II Furfan de Ros and the other effigies were crushed and driven down into the basement. Very luckily a Bronze Casting of Robert II's Effigy was in Victoria and Albert Museum, so that a replica Effigy could be re-carved to replace the Nazi broken deRos Effigy.

Chapter 12
Misfire

I locate the Northbound Train Station back to Leeds. Hop on and off we go.

During the train ride they have a TV News station on. Dailey News, it is June 14th, 2017.

A Royal Tank Regiment Tank has blown up during a Live Fire Practice.

I had a couple of hours to sit with that piece of Information. I watch as the TV News anchors discuss this Terrible Event. I get a Taxi from the Train Station back to Mick's house.

In I go with dread. Would Mick know? Should I tell him if he doesn't? I asked him "If he knew about the Live Fire Accident with a Tank?
He had.

"Do you know what happened, Mick?"
"I have a pretty good guess," Mick says.

Seems Mick's job in the RTR when not Piping was Instruction of Proper Loading and Firing of Ordinance in Tanks.

Yes, I guess he probably knows exactly what happened. He starts discussing the procedures of Loading and Firing of a Tank. He can see on my face that I am interested but I am not understanding the terminology he is using.

I am watching his face closely. His face is not that of an older man with Cancer. He is now a 30-year-old Sergeant who is an Instructor for the Handling of Tank Ordinance.

He has changed into a young guy in front of my eyes...

"Wait here," Mick commands.
He dashes upstairs and jogs back down the very steep stairway loaded with Binders of Instructions that he used as an Officer.
He is not feeling the Aches and Pains of an hour before. He is in Military Instructor Mode. I sat back amazed at his transformation; clearly this military training had been so drilled into his subconsciousness that it snapped back-on like a switch.

I didn't say a word that is not about Tank's Ordinance.
I watch awestruck at what I am seeing. He is so into describing every detail about the "Wad". How heavy it is. He is describing to me as if I am a new Recruit he needs to teach.
Details, Details, Details...

He gets out his computer so that I can see exactly what parts he is talking about. He makes sure that I, as the "new recruit", understands every aspect of what he is teaching.
Next, he teaches me about Misfire.

What to do if a Misfire occurs. I am to drive my tank away from other tanks, buildings, and soldiers, how many yards I would need to be away from everything.

I would have a time clock I would need to start; the Clock is for 30 minutes. Do not move, do not open the hatch, do nothing but sit tight. 30 minutes.

"Why 30 minutes, Mick?"
"If you open the hatch, oxygen will rush in and the ordinance would be activated, the Tank will blow up."
He describes how each man would die in this explosion by where they are seated in the Tank.

He is not trying to scare me as a woman, he is teaching his "new recruit", how NOT to die in a Tank Misfire.

Sitting there watching him I now could see why his men respected him as an officer.

I got to witness it firsthand.

I never mentioned this evening's events to Mick ever again.
It was mine to keep and look back on when I need reassurance that people are good.

From a Silly Lovable Rake to a Cold and Cool Leader in War Time. Cementing my thoughts as to why Mick's "Soldiers Absolutely Adored Him."

Calm in the face of Danger, Care of his Men but Light and Carefree in the Music Arena, with a need to Win with his Pipe Band, foremost.

P.S. Mick was right with his conclusion of what happened at the Live Fire Tank Explosion in 2017. A few years later the Military's Findings of the Explosion. Reasons was just as described to me in 2017, by Mick.

Chapter 13
Under Water Detonation

Kirkham Abbey is on our schedule for the next day. Mick has morphed back to his current Cancer ridden self again from last night.

It is a drizzly day but not bad. We bundle up and are off on a new adventure. Mick is now totally immersed in my research of the de Ros Family. As far as he is concerned, since he was a Royal Tank Regiment Officer who wears Rose Hunting Tartan, he too is a "Card Carrying" member of the Rose Family of Kilravock too. He smiles as he says that to me outside the gates of Kirkham Abbey. Another Abbey that was built by the de Ros Family.

Yet again this Abbey is in ruins a la Henry VIII. Sad. But Beautiful. We looked over the site. There are signs posted looking towards the river that runs by this site. A picture of **Winston Churchill** looking at the same view as us. The river looks deeper in the picture than it was on the day while we were there.

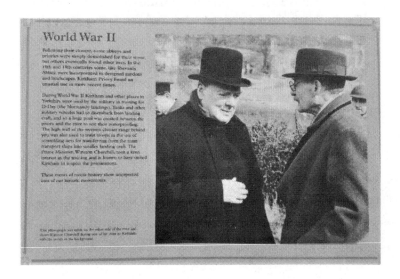

The Arch Front Gate of Kirkham Abbey with Trois Bouts D'Leau showing.

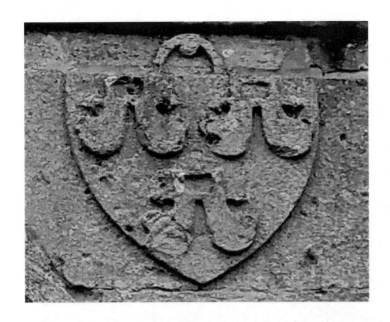

Look for the Bullet holes on this Trois Bouts D'
L'eau Heraldry on the front Archway of Kirkham
Abbey.
Remember being bored as a teenager? Good
thing you didn't have a rifle...

We read the sign, in WWII; Kirkham Abbey was where the Military learned to Detonate Under Water Ordinance. Underwater explosions were a new thing then. So, practice makes perfect, using the dammed-up river next to the Kirkham Abbey grounds was just the place to be. Out of the way from people's homes and businesses.

We wandered back out the front gate and looked at the Trois Bouts D'Leau Heraldry of the deRos's on the Arch two of them, one on each side of the entry arch.

The Trois Bouts D'Leau Heraldry to this day is still used by the Duke of Rutland of England and the Roses of Kilravock. Carved into the Stonework Arch of the front gate of Kirkham Abbey.

Funny though Mick points out what looks to be bullet holes in the Heraldry. Like some men during WWII got bored waiting on the Underwater Bombs, took a few pot shots at the Arches.

The bullet holes are still visible today.

Really, he had a sharp eye still and a very good sense of humor. He knew those holes were made by bored young men who were not being supervised.

Chapter 14
Belvoir Abbey

Mick had found on a map Belvoir Castle in Grantham, in Nottinghamshire England. Belvoir Castle also had belonged to the de Ros Family. The only remaining English Castle that had been owned by Robert II Furfan de Ros, not to have been blown into smithereens. The de Ros Family had gained the title to Belvoir Castle in Robert II Furfan de Ros's father Edvard de Ros' lifetime.

Belvoir Castle Located in Grantham in Nottinghamshire England.

A funny but sad thing about Belvoir Castle and the Manners Family. The word Belvoir is obviously a French Word for "Beautiful View". The English Aristocracy for hundreds of years only spoke French. Not English. Over the years the pronunciation of the word Belvoir was changed to "Beaver." Beaver Castle. I have watched the Duchess of Rutland on camera say "Beaver" Castle instead of pronouncing the name of the Castle Belvoir.

I am rather insulted as a Rose that the pronunciation has been bastardized in such a manner. Oh! Yes, I just typed a pun.

It is still inhabited by the Manners Family who are related to the de Ros family and uses the Trois Bouts D'Leau Heraldry of de Ros same as the Scottish Roses of Kilravock. The de Ros Family mid 1400's didn't have a male heir; the daughter married an Earl by the name of Manners.

FYI there was a split of the de Ros/Rose of Kilravock family line. In 1258 Robert II Furfan de Ros' son William III de Ros and his grandson Robert IV deRos journey to Strathnairn, Scotland to visit their Scottish Lands.

Lands given to Robert II Furfan de Ros as the Bride's Marriage Portion from King William the Lion of Scotland when Robert II Furfan de Ros married Isabela MacWilliam, King William the Lion's Daughter.

That's right Robert II Furfan de Ros married a Scottish Princess.
How do you say, "Power and Control" in a different way?

Say this word out loud, "Royalty."

Seems there was a child that stayed up in Scotland after the visit. As William III de Ros and (his first-born son) Robert IV de Ros, both guys had first-born sons back in England and were both married. One of those two guys left behind an illegitimate child (Conjecture). That child grows up to be Hugh 1st de Ros of Kilravock Scotland with the exact same de Ros Heraldry the Trois Bouts D'Leau as that specific line of de Ros' of England.
This little piece of information was lost to the end of time as they didn't want to acknowledge this tiny little fact named Hugh.
That occurrence is just not recognized, ever. There was a claim that the birth certificate for Hugh I deRos had been burned in the fire, years later in Elgin Cathedral. Very Convenient.
Local to Kilravock Castle is the ruins of Elgin Cathedral that had been burned down by the Wolf of Badenoch, Alexander Stewart. The second son of Robert II Bruce. (1343-1405)
A very convenient way to cover up was that there was no paperwork for a Bastard child.

Wink Wink.

Any which way of it, William III de Ros or Robert IV de Ros left a male heir in Scotland.

This is my conjecture as to how a Male Heir appears at Kilravock Scotland bearing the Trois Bouts D'Leau Heraldry still used to this day.

What is important about the Robert II Furfan de Ros Heraldry is that it was not the original de Ros Heraldry. No. It belonged to the de Payens family prior to it being given to Robert II Furfan de Ros' father Edvard de Ros.

That's right, the dePayens Family as in,
Hugh dePayens the First Grand Master of the Knights Templar.

The First Knights Templar Grand Master, Hugh dePayens who was Robert II Furfan de Ros' actual Great Uncle. Yes.

Did I Mention "Power and Control"?

I did absolutely.

That heraldry and family connection is only through that specific Robert II Furfan de Ros family line. None of his de Ros brothers used the Trois Bouts d'Leau heraldry, Period.

Chapter 15
Spital Inn

During the day of my train ride down to London and back, Mick had time to work on other places for us to visit.

I had told Mick that the United States' first President, George Washington was a direct line descendant of Robert II Furfan de Ros. So, he researched the Washington/Wessington family of Selby, England.

So off we go to visit Selby Abbey, a specific religious house for the Washington/Wessington family. The reason for the two spellings as standardization of spelling did not occur until the mid-1400's so then there are the two versions of the Washington name.

On route to Selby Abbey, we drive past a motel type business called "The Spital Inn."

"**Stop** go back, turn around Mick, I need a picture!" I scream.

"Mick says Susan, you are insane!"

"Look here Tank Commander turn this little car around, now!" I Order! Laughingly.

"You want me to turn around so you can take a picture of that building?" says Mick, not believing me.

"Yes, you have the ability to turn this tiny car around and drive back, Correct?" I say with fake righteous indignation.

"Goodness what I must do to please you!" chuckled Mick.

We got on just like the old friends that we were. Really why would you name your business, "The Spital Inn?"

I have the picture to prove it.

Chapter 16
George Washington

We arrive at the town of Selby, I had no knowledge of this place as it was concerning the U.S. President George Washington, a man I had not researched anything about, other than he is The First of the United States. President Washington who was a Direct Line Descendant of Robert II Furfan de Ros.

We enter the Abbey; it has stained glass windows surrounding the entire top portion of the walls. There is a Docent that greets us, to show us around. They notice my American Accent; they guide us directly to the Washington Stain Glass Window. It's an image of the Washington Family Heraldry. Three Stars and Red and White Stripes. WOW It looks so American. I have seen this heraldry before. The very top center window is the Washington Heraldry.

The Washington Family-Stained Glass Window

Mick is so excited to show me this. It seems that Benjamin Franklin, yes **"The, Benjamin Franklin"** had seen George Washington's Heraldry. Mr. Franklin approached George Washington to use his Heraldry for the Medals to be given to U.S. Military Soldiers wounded in the line of duty.

America's Purple Heart.

The Heraldry was also the source of the U.S. Flag also, a la Benjamin Franklin. Mick was so proud of his finding the Washington Heraldry Connection to de Ros, The American Stars and Stripes Flag and The U.S. Purple Heart.

Mick's source of Pride was that he was be able to add to the History of "His Clan" Family named Rose of Kilravock, Scotland.
Aaaah, My Heart.

On to Belvoir Castle. We arrive at Belvoir Castle; we park in the lot designated. But we are met by an attendant that says that the castle was closed due to family obligations. Seems the Manners Family who live in the Castle were mid divorce as was headlined in the British Media. We never guessed that it would close the tours of the castle itself.

On the way back we discussed other pictures of Mick. The picture of you shaking hands with the Queen and her Secretary on a field.

"You are smiling Broadly. Not typical for the UK Military."
"I saw no reason to not smile, the Queen was smiling at me." Fair enough.

The picture of you with, I think, the Queen's sister Margaret. Is the next picture. The Officer that is standing next to you. Looks to be upset.
Mick "Yes, I answered all of Margaret's Questions. We had a conversation."

If a person High Born, or low asked a question of me while I was in Uniform, I felt I was Honor Bound to politely answer each and every question presented to me with a smile.
Again, Fair enough.

Back to another wonderful Thanksgiving Dinner, which could not be beat. And a night at the pub with old friends.

Chapter 17
Departure

The day of departure arrives for me. To think that I would never be able to speak in person with this kind man in a few short months, broke my heart.

He would be gone, forever. I was visibly shaken, the Taxi ride to the Northbound Train Station was quiet, not our usual friendly conversation.

I could not bring myself to speak.

Years later, I am right now crying as I type as if it is happening again today.

We exited the Taxi. Mick was standing very Tall as an Officer. He walked/marched me to my gate. He turned and faced me, I hugged him, then stood back thinking he would say something.

He stood back at attention. He looked sharp and steady at my face, then my entire body then back up to my face.

He was memorizing me. He knew he was dying soon, he wanted to have a proper mental picture of me to keep. He didn't say another word to me. We had already said everything there was to say. He motioned to me to get on the train. I chose a window seat close to where he was standing. He was still staring at my face.
He did so, until the train pulled out.

I burst into tears that would not stop. The Scottish grandmothers on that train came to console me. "What is wrong Darling?"

I just said goodbye to a close friend for the last time, he will be dying in about 6 months, and I am going back to California where I live.

Not to see him again.

Those consoling Scottish Grandmothers were Angels! Dressed as Scottish terrorists in floral print cotton dresses and sweaters.

It's not the story I was sent to get. It was the story that happened.

We lived a Lifetime in Ten Days.

Photograph Credits

Page 12 Susan Rose   "Bingley Arms"
Page 18 Susan Rose "Rievaulx Grinding Stone"
Page 19 Susan Rose   "The End of Monastic"
Page 20 Susan Rose   " Stone Peacock"
Page 21 Susan Rose   "The Rievaulx Arches"
Page 23 Susan Rose "Helmsley Metal Vikings"
Page 24 Susan Rose   "Stone Cannon Ball"
Page 25 Susan Rose   "Robert de Roos"
Page 25 Susan Rose "Helmsley Back Entrance"
Page 26 Susan Rose   "Helmsley Window"
Page 27 Susan Rose   "Scarborough Village"
Page 28 Susan Rose   "Scarborough Castle"
Page 30 Provided by RTR   "Lady Elizabeth"
Page 31 Provided by RTR   "Painting of Pipe Sargent"
Page 32 Provided by RTR "Tank with Chinese Eyes"
Page 33 Provided by RTR   "Mick with the Mermaid"
Page 34 Provided by RTR "Mick front of Tank"
Page 35 Provided by RTR   "On tour in South America"
Page 37 Wikipedia   "Leeds Royal Armory on River"
Page 38 Susan Rose   "The River Aire"
Page 38 Susan Rose   "Family Canal Boat"
Page 39 Susan Rose "Two men on an elephant"
Page 40 Susan Rose   "Mounted Horses"
Page 41 Susan Rose   "Battle of Agincourt"
Page 41 Susan Rose   "Painting of Agincourt"

Page 42 Susan Rose "Picture of Painting of John Lord Roos"

Page 43 Susan Rose "List of Names Agincourt Sign"

Page 44 Susan Rose "Looking up the Weapon Tower"

Page 45 Susan Rose "Henry VIII Helmet"

Page 50 Provided by RTR "Juicy Bits"

Page 59 Uncredited "Child Mick in Kilt & Scots Guards"

Page 60 Provided by RTR "Clan Rose Highland Dancers"

Page 61 Susan Rose "Whitby Abbey"

Page 62 Susan Rose "Robinhood's Bay"

Page 65 Susan Rose "Round of Temple Church"

Page 66 Susan Rose "Top Half of Effigy"

Page 67 Public Domain "Very Old Etching of Robert"

Page 89 Susan Rose " Real Life Effigy"

Page 76 Susan Rose "Winston Churchill"

Page 77 Susan Rose "Arch of Kirkham"

Page 78 Susan Rose "Trois Bouts D'Leau"

Page 78 Susan Rose "Mick at Kirkham"

Page 81 Susan Rose "Belvoir"

Page 86 Susan Rose "The Spital Inn"

Page 87 Susan Rose "Selby Abbey"

Page 88 Susan Rose "Washington Stained Glass"

Page 89 Wikipedia "U.S. Purple Heart"

Page 90 Provided by RTR "Mick with The Queen"

Page 91 Provided by RTR "Mick with Margaret"

Made in the USA
Columbia, SC
23 May 2024

35674237R00059